T0290799

Quirks & Quillets

Quirks

&

Quillets

Karen Mac Cormack

CHAX PRESS ■ TUCSON 1991

Copyright © 1991 to Karen Mac Cormack

All rights reserved. Neither this book, nor any part thereof, may be reproduced or transmitted in any form or by any means unless with the express written permission of the publisher.

This publication has been made possible in part through the generous support of the Tucson/Pima Arts Council, Bookman's Used Books, and the Chax Press Members.

Printed by Cushing-Malloy, Inc., of Ann Arbor, Michigan.

Published by Chax Press, 101 West Sixth Street, no. 4, Tucson, Arizona 85701 USA.

Library of Congress Cataloging-in-Publication Data
Mac Cormack, Karen, 1956-
    Quirks & quillets / Karen Mac Cormack.
       p.   cm.
    ISBN 0-925904-04-X : $8.00
    I. Title II. Title: Quirks and quillets.
    PR9199.3.M23Q57   1991
  811'.54--dc20   90-48158
                                           CIP

ISBN 0-925904-04-X

for Stephen

Toronto • San Diego • Toronto

1989

Difference makes its conquests even in such matters as pin-heads.

— Susan Hicks Beach, *The Yesterdays Behind the Door*

The untried decibel of seamless hose unhurried sentence its adjectives the chosen ladder geological manoeuvre or landing strip spangles the same man connected *paillettes* cramp the page's reproduction not ours or the level's pinafore before piano trudging words ahead of their names an algebra of what is scene momentous underneath.

One over in easy boots glow here or where glamour stays the fluid always empties before silk reached Europe November was originally the ninth month through impluvia liquids that are non-elastic recur as *interval* numerals conform to the space of their names on paper the ventricle looks different doubt remains delays the same.

Not rhythm yet repetition she said so it was written to be recorded but if heard then listened to attentively without false moves or the maximum number of pauses in an attention span's treble clef folds on a number the back lot serpentine telling a choir this voice.

Coronation knot black and yellow lace diversion a stocking doesn't retain shape of leg tracery substitution or so much framing won't lie in wait the means of stretch Topkapi what continues to fascinate rows over us in aspiration our disguises amplify gravity affords the difference between what's overheard underfoot and the rent's always due as a beginning again.

Combination or weaving the influence of *literature* on sunsets with a proven space for heaving anything at all through windows where aeroplane numbers are without temperature small pressed dates frustrate hedonism how far off this or thus imposed.

Pause of temple nothing vague about the
word *consequences* to visit son first a father
to daughter's index or candour for a later
man fewer than March of thirty one now
plus two windmills notwithstanding
evidence or even affection for the name of
river woodland and large geese feathered
by percentages those small chance meetings
crooned.

A plaster *likeness* admiration comatose suggestion elevate overdrive swarm ventifact and unlucky hour wanting ready hover understood at reveal or too much biennial stubborn permit lodging clay sand a high wind wide the product at glance curtains in.

The visibility of oncoming foil there are rudimentary icons to reflect the blindman's holiday *far enough* in unknown quantity involves speed not catching up to a name this nod at grace the apex of eyes do not resume sight on opening a triangular motion to honour the bridge in all these particulars.

Parcels *are* since the act of wrapping was made famous to the inexplicable more or less by chance warranty without calculator or transverse magnet impinging upon a redness when FIDO isn't the dog so much more century the *nocturne's* inventor recently eighteenth and with string.

Somehow this did not mean the shortest distance between two points in the answer most closely related to the question set in antique forms more lavish than attention on such an occasion can engender words remembered or renewed a force of specialty as yours to recognize not in so many this much arrival went.

Bright partition on the way to a painting leans on a loan bricks minus cement lessen the load we contract no promise is ten years valid parking lapse background the constant was dimensional negation shoes for triptych driving solid threadbare knuckles separatist.

To make sensual what is public freed from socks the creaking of the floor every sort of punctual on the morning those looking both ways for Sunday observe our own mark of rehearsal four apart well known the running is not a place of post to which replies.

The hands move as turntable demonstrable if purpose is three hundred and sixty five and activity a division of 8 into heaven with goal a variable and concentration determined by six to 9 out of twenty four occasionally including or allowing 60 on the run and five standing if more sitting still less production the brink must be accounted for anything.

Cruelty a makeshift shelter exquisite object precisely in its centre though not origami creases are numerous paper a line cut or burgeoning there's more to this than sample relics bird songstress stuttering a limestone path dark throat catches in the dawn pinned to somewhere else *possess*.

Any and all that isn't this surrogate spelling
of wing-span and method for decoding the
night a plural darkness slender sliver
suture as things consecutive partake of
motion the seat on the plane preceded by
form of payment selection of writing
instrument cut cloth bone and bracelet
leather or not description of enclosed heat
diaphanous hearing *de*parted *in*vented slow
singular source juice in the trademark
pealing lively crisp white simulation and
go.

Terse garret or kissing crust pages wander also the smallest sort of pin moveables *are* of value for example peak flicker a drinking glass to crowd for caravan bare the bell at cupboard love speak gently and give the office not in pothooks and hangers sight in ridge or even *rouleau* release the paper let what will happen edge.

Is the assertion of geography the proliferation of accents within an expanding language hence this weather in some places at any time of year it's easier to remember the sun rises than when the umbrella went missing incorporation of onslaught without proven technique everyone's least favourite critic teaching the newspaper to read who's paid for this is someone else from the telephone directory listing any way into port.

Harlequin infantry they turn as on an axis these gestures doubling themselves to fullness reach an architecture studies don't prepare one any better for coronary arrest there's whiteness in between however long the wishbone hours *fabliau* and cyclone outruns cello.

Double capacity dynamic for days although wearing masks as protection until under and around fumes bargain the next capacity included planning that's across the garden someone doesn't land-of-made-in-believe or a colourized film on a black and white television the free depictions of living so much closer to the equator a thinner ocean stretch of brave as ever more glistening libido glance.

On a species not static in daily three-dimensional script ensign of what is much larger than a paragraph lagoon beside the sunshine placing combinations on a page so much lift and lucid position intervention can be that where the sand ends encouraged growth cut back to acknowledge different spellings.

This curious release of leaves the fugue among us delivered a personal number of hindsight currency restricts an ingenuity recorded in France while television insults anyone two more keys enclose space within time so shells appear smoother on the counter of any slide into that wall between partitions current is infused forgers in formation.

Sweeping the variations a moment of approximate sphere urges the plane along time for anything to reach table flushing grids are common in some way crops shape the elsewhere occupied needles health derives its singular strands fluid clear circle through.

To salivate would rust the metal simulated grain intervenes a flag pole comparison to order independence day aside the sky in what three countries represented forestry arrives on the pure extracted use of water stops clarification for all the world to see incision a number which shelf on an early price belief is location the conveyance pays to this removal instrument a human extension swimsuits in part column post haste.

Version bellhop less answer no question of east interior soothsayer saturate ice predicate deal nine of his name her letters the next moment same day feverfew penchant yes please paragraph membership and weakness tropopause.

When closed without penalty leave ahead video entertainment as indicated along this route from feature-length passengers assistance open connecting symbols and abbreviations in sleeping reference operates daily between transferring the performance allotted in deluxe carry identification of any compliments entry provides and crossing in part withdraws to/from points south.

In this way the body translates to taste or smell compared for lack of equilibrium the drum skin fine it is what doing does when termination incites ingenuity so firm surfaces to lean on are factors in a different sight windshield wipers pursue warrant no fortune rhapsody in the bolder clauses a scare surge or mallet conveyance bitten sleek inquiry forgetting the wait extend.

Assigned *blue* water is clear conception's more than that could show fox prints early in the *h*'s night swift owl or surly bands signal the impression wind before window whatever that means to the letter or hue a cry ring slips in patter as the crow flys an arm will not be long nor loud enough near the fingers a position of stone time on a table where these words as architraves place *meant* portcullis loop resumes dot histories.

For root to evade stock answer on the go in a driverless adjacence named after more dependency austere when young credential especially for the serious half an hour's no call for the man's *will work for food* lottery pilgrimage of some in waking the walls suggest resurface available for more of us have not done so enclosed.

As directed just under the product along with your light strokes the preferred shaping start satisfied or material with reason how conductors interfere with the view a posse undertakes plain right ruin on Thursday a complacency with optional flinches limbs depressions launched early local values the wire is this future delicate between the legs a term enjoyed broom sandcastle full splash for not stable.

These patterns afford the loquacious a
dividend pink peonies smell larger than the
room is not circuitous a run burned over
where perhaps even weather has a dialect
of absorption cells aren't sex the rifle kills a
single battery runs on and neither comes
equipped with legs.

Prominence muster trousers for the cooler of it ends down the road moor siphon electricity interprets this earth pebbles lair yesterday bleached if cordial pass upstream yolk contained spreading marked handwriting larger towards the middle less self-conscious assonance cuffs deformed a frame but it's picture varnish drumming no view withstood an hour of done to fasten or pertain logging was a science too.

As on a murmur the fluid inside crest an uncertain inhalation mole raises ballast for what isn't home out-creased role turns in side stepping stop the lathe I am of flesh you no ground given mammal for a nearer search this white these hungers form from name to name less gradual about contrast pulling the maroon down ventil.

Increased honey towards acquaintance seeps to memory for another time place oneself in union splits hour from day sighs are not the weariest tone of fall apart the absent secrecy's measure of yield goes before the *yes* faded against all other descriptions grounded shock *rubati* of to see was spoken for sweet knowing reinforced the letters act.

As a landscape falters from the steering of eye not stopping at point rather plain scabbard the gravel heat loose in one's hand over metal there's fanbelt service counter part of glaze goes too much for the weather watch the news chipped notice in rear view blade edge.

Sawdust a partial stop to events childhood sideways men of straw untwisted central downmost isotherm undertow basement of either attendance silt omission conjunction of tangent facial grade antidote recursion formula vendetta suspense applicable street frequency over.

Tomahawk entry letterhead on white
ground the chair back upright slang palace
a foot in its turns for the worse parole
strains not a printer's face golden smoke
and the fire blew anchors town listing
arrow slope buttons converge to cycle sleep
is not commodity refrain scale rally and
swoop file the listless sever.

The speeches in privacy without swallowing the tongs a taste of supper words ignite between a jumble lush and later so the sound abandoned lungs to match the eyes pale fading simply within or building overall the gait goes over the tie image of smell spread robust other to anxious leaf tucked vein suppose a slice dismantled the floorboards or steps material order of disaster hunger imported to self true or no leasing the air beyond release.

And in the letter numerals not far behind down sealing wax or country road the appointment an anxiety of example within corpus a body's spelling mistakes one on another dialling so the number is *wrong* if the blank sheet fell behind the hair ahead characteristics intoxicate purloin advantage to take a piece of cutlery foreign usage exact rainfall against spool without absorption carnage recycled stretch.

Foregoing impartial likeness threads drop where the thermometer left off it only matters to someone else that the door is closed upon leaving for now the proliferation of exits is grief enough arms in these leaves drying an open solitude in increments the belief that there's paint on walls paintings patching anomalies or marbles in the mouth a fast-growing background attention span in the form of everyday objects of a given culture basting corrects this sink is full.

All passage fall lean-to diction paralyse the driven on their day off the going rate abided splice fail or parched grip a walk of more than twenty paces from premeditated surprise conform to stagger impasse inkless paces regain the gone around this threw.

Karen Mac Cormack's previous books are *Quill Driver* (Nightwood Editions, 1989), *Straw Cupid* (Nightwood, 1987), and *Nothing by Mouth* (Underwhich Editions, 1984). Her work was also included in the 1986 anthology *Into the Nightlife* (Nightwood). Born in Africa, she is a Canadian citizen living in Toronto, and, in addition to her work as a writer, has produced video art works and worked extensively in publishing.

Quirks & Quillets has been designed and typeset by Charles Alexander, using a Northgate computer, employing Ventura Publisher software, and printing camera ready copy with a Hewlett Packard Laserjet III printer with Postscript cartridge. The typeface is Palatino, with a title-page and cover display ampersand of Zapf Chancery. The cover drawing is by Cynthia Miller.

Chax Press publishes books in editions which explore the possibilities of the art of the book, and in literary trade paperback editions. We also sponsor many events in our own community in an attempt to build a vibrant vortex of literary and related activities. Other literary trade editions from Chax Press include the following books.

Eli Goldblatt, *Sessions*. 1991. $9.

Sheila Murphy, *Teth*. 1991. $9

Charles Alexander, *Hopeful Buildings*. 1990. $9.95.

Larry Evers and Felipe S. Molina, eds., *Wo'i Bwikam/ Coyote Songs*. 1990. $8.

bpNichol, *Art Facts: A Book of Contexts*. 1990. $15.

Chax has also, since 1984, published more than a dozen books in handmade book arts editions, including works by Charles Bernstein, Paul Metcalf, Anne Kingsbury, Karl Young, Lyn Hejinian, Kit Robinson, and many others. Forthcoming books from Chax Press include works by Ron Silliman, Beverly Dahlen, Leslie Scalapino, Norman Fischer, and more.